WHAT FILLS YOU, CONTROLS YOU

Walter Masocha

authorHOUSE®

AuthorHouse™ UK Ltd.
1663 Liberty Drive
Bloomington, IN 47403 USA
www.authorhouse.co.uk
Phone: 0800.197.4150

Published by AuthorHouse 05/28/2014

ISBN: 978-1-4969-7992-6 (sc)
ISBN: 978-1-4969-7993-3 (hc)
ISBN: 978-1-4969-7994-0 (e)

Contents

Acknowledgements

As always, my first acknowledgements go to the Lord God almighty, who gave me the inspiration to write this book with much reference to His written Word. Secondly, I would like to express my special thanks and appreciation to my lovely, beautiful wife Judith, who endured my many sleepless nights and weeks away from home as I wrote yet another book. I thank her for her understanding and support in many ways, in particular, her prayers. She is such a blessing to me. I never cease to thank God for my mother, the God-fearing woman who carried me in her womb and nurtured me from the day I was born. My thanks also go to my dearest children, Sandra and Jeffrey, Sharon, Tinashe and Tafadzwa, my beloved 'adopted' children, David and Tsungayi Caroline (Joy), as well as my brothers and sisters who supported me in different ways. Last but not least, I extend my thanks to all the saints and leadership of the church Agape for All Nations Ministries International, who also encouraged me to publish my writings and messages/sermons, and also supported me through prayers. God's blessings to you all.

Dedication

I dedicate this book to all the children of God world-wide, and in particular to my brother, John Masocha and his wife, Sophia.

CHAPTER ONE

Introduction

This book is about behaviour. It's about actions. In it I try to explain the underlying causes of human actions and behaviour. I try to do this not from a psychological or philosophical perspective. It's not Christian Ethics either. I claim no knowledge on these and many other areas of human endeavour. I try to make it simple for those of us who are not initiated in such fields of learning. I try to explain it from a Biblical point of view. By Biblical I do not mean Theological. I mean I just use simple passages from the Bible to demonstrate the source and causes of some of our responses as Christians, our actions and/or reactions, and our attitudes too. When someone 'bursts out' or 'loses it' or 'explodes', or suddenly just goes quiet, moody, or commits suicide, what would have happened? What causes a balloon to explode? What causes a tyre to burst? What causes rivers and dams to spill over . . . something people call 'flooding'?

I admit there is fallacy in generalisations, but in this book allow me to generalise. I propose a ONE-LINE answer to all these scenarios—Whether man or creature, plant, animal, birds, or nature _ whatever fills you, controls you! If you want to know the reason why people, nature, animals and other creatures behave the way they do, just check out what they are full of. Once you get to grips with what they are full of, I propose in this book that the end result is pretty much predictable. For the sake of size of the book, I shall limit my analysis to the human species, and in particular those who are in that segment of religion called Christianity. I use these as a case study, or a sample. But I believe that the main thesis of this book is applicable to all mankind, and indeed all of God's creation. It is true: What fills you, controls you. I am sure you will agree with me as we pick a few examples in this book. Come with me.

If you will, let us start with the passage of scripture in **Mark 7:20-23**[1]. It says:

> 20 *And he said, That which cometh out of the man, that defileth the man.* 21 *For from within, out of the heart of men, proceed evil thoughts, adulteries, fornications, murders,* 22 *Thefts, covetousness, wickedness, deceit, lasciviousness, an evil eye, blasphemy, pride, foolishness:* 23 *All these evil things come from within, and defile the man.*

1 Most of the Bible passages quoted in this book were sourced from www.**kingjamesbible**online.org

You see what Jesus Christ was saying here? It confirms my basic point. What we see a human being doing or even saying to themselves or to others is only a function of what is 'within' the person. Check out the list of things in verses 21 and 22. Would you say none of these affect you. If any of these is relevant to you, then you need this book.

Proverbs 14:12 says:

> 12 *There is a way which seemeth right unto a man, but the end thereof are the ways of death.*

Again, these are words of wisdom from one who had 'been there, done that and got a T-shirt!' Before you say or do anything, check out what you are full of. That's wisdom. It will save you a lot of pain and trouble in the future. You know what I am saying?

Many people have done things they regret. Perhaps you have too, and like everyone else, you wonder what happened, or how it happened. I find the answer in **John 10:10**. The thief came. You know, thieves do not announce when they will come. They do not advertise in newspapers, on radio or television to pre-warn you that they are coming. They take a leaf from their father, the devil. Check out **John 10:10**. It says:

> 10 *The thief cometh not, but for to steal, and to kill, and to destroy: I am come that they might have life, and that they might have it more abundantly.*

I have no doubt you know who is referred to as the thief. This verse summarises mission statements of two kings. Part (a) sums up the mission of the enemy on God's children. Part (b) sums up the mission of our Lord and Saviour, Jesus Christ. The verse sums up the missions of two opposing governments or kingdoms—the Kingdom of the devil on the one hand, and the Kingdom of God on the other. It's up to you which government or kingdom you want to belong to. Either government or kingdom lands you in an environment or territory that fills you up with stuff. Stuff that will surely control you and dictate your character, language and behaviour. It could be information; what you hear; what you see etc. Whatever the kingdom or government of your choice offers you, you are sure to be full. And as I have already said . . . **whatever** fills you, controls you. Or would you rather I put it this way: **whoever** fills you, controls you. I don't know about you, but in the context of **John 10:10**, I choose life. Abundant life. I choose the Kingdom of God. Whatever that government offers, I want to be full of it. Don't you?

An Illustration

It's a true saying: whatever fills you controls you. Consider the following illustration. Take two water glasses and put them in a tray, then place the tray on a level surface—say a table. Fill one of them with orange juice. Fill the other glass with water. Yeah? Ok. Now, gently shake the glass that's full of orange juice. Check what comes out. Orange juice, right? Now do the same for the glass that's full of water. What comes out? Water, of-course! Well, so what's the point? Ah, you don't get it? Well, here it is: When circumstances of life shake you (as they will surely do throughout your life), you spill out only that which you are full of!

When you hear people saying: 'I don't know where my behaviour came from', or 'I have no idea why I acted the way I did'; that's a lie. They just spilled out what they were full of. The trouble is that some people don't quite know what they are full of, until something happens that really shakes them. Here is another example I borrowed from my other book on the Threshing Floor[2]. Read on.

A tree without wasps (*Muti usina mago/Isihlahla esingela lonyovu*)

Consider the following episode. When I was young, growing up in the village in Buhera, Zimbabwe, I used to be a shepherd boy. Myself and boys from the neighbourhood used to take our animals for grazing every day, and we would sometimes meet up for company. One day as I was looking for a lamb that had sort of strayed away, I squatted under a small tree to shield myself from the scorching sun. As I sat there, I suddenly saw one small boy running, screaming so loudly and scratching his head like crazy.

---

2 THRESHING FLOOR D.I.Y STYLE: A New Approach For A New Generation; From Harvest to Seed. Dr. Walter Masocha. Aug. 2013. pp. 74-76 (Trafford Publishing). I strongly recommend this book to every child of God who is serious about their relationship with the Lord.

He ran towards me because I was a little older than him. I covered him in my arms as he continued to cry aloud.

Eventually I calmed him down. I asked why he was crying. He told me that he had sort of shaken one of the shrubs and then got stung by wasps. When I looked at his face, sure enough, the evidence was there for anyone to see. He had a swollen upper eye and a shiny, swollen lower lip. The wasps had stung him real good. I had had many such experiences before. I knew the feeling. I knew the pain the young man was going through. As I comforted him, I suddenly began to fear, just in case there were some wasps up in the tree I was squatting under! Something told me to check it out by shaking the trunk of the tree. It was small enough. We were not stung. There were no wasps. The young boy had been stung twice. He had shaken the small tree or shrub/bush. I then went and expertly destroyed the wasp nest by attacking it with my catapult, from a small distance of-course. I saw the wasps scattering away, their home destroyed. They flew away in different directions, never again to return to that tree. If any other small boy shook the same tree the next day, they would not be stung.

As I wrote this book, now an adult based in Scotland, UK, the Holy Spirit reminded me of that unfortunate episode, and of similar encounters I personally had with wasps, way back in my humble beginnings in the village. The Lord said that the boy was stung because he had shaken a tree/shrub in which wasps had their nest. Meanwhile, when I shook the tree I was squatting under, I was not stung for a very simple reason—there was no wasp nest up that tree, therefore no wasps. No wasps in the tree, no one gets stung. No wasps, no sting. If you get stung, it means there are wasps in the tree, even if you don't immediately see their nest.

Then the Lord asked me to examine my own life tree and see if there are any wasps that suddenly sting others. If I sting others in my speech, it means there are wasps in me. I would need the catapult of the Word of God to scatter the wasp nest in me. The wasp nest refers to the root causes of a sharp tongue. People 'snap' at others because of anger, bitterness or just mere rudeness. When you get rid of these at the threshing floor, you find that you do not sting other children of God.

If you shake a tree without wasps, no wasps come out. In my vernacular language they would say it this way: "*Muti usina mago, ukazunzwa, haubudisi mago*" "*or "Isihlahla esingela lonyovu, ungasi nyikinyisa, asiphumi lonyovu*". Say the same in your mother tongue, if English is not your first language. I am sure you will understand the deeper meaning of it[3]. What am I saying here? If people get stung, it means there are wasps around. The tree is full of wasps. People will not know, until somebody shakes the tree! *Hokoyo*! *Basopo lo!*

Well . . . you get the point, don't you? Whatever fills you, controls you.

This book takes a closer look at a few (key) things that fill people, with repercussions or consequences that are far-reaching at times. I mean, people get really full! *Kuita kuzara*!

---

3 I have come to realise that if things are said in one's native language, they tend to be grasped or understood better and quicker. So even in my preaching or sermons, if I go to countries whose first language or mother tongue is not English, I like to throw in a word or two in the native language. Often, I do that in the UK too. The response is always tremendous. My prayer is that one day this book shall be translated into many languages other than English, to benefit Christians all over the world.

Chapter 2 looks at Pregnancy, while Chapter 3 discusses the effects of being filled with Drink and Drugs. Chapter 4 looks at Bitterness and Anger, and Chapter 5 looks at what happens when people are full of Jealousy and Hatred. Chapter 6 analyses the after-effects of Love in its various forms or types, while Chapter 7 analyses what happens when people are full of evil spirits or full of the Holy Spirit. Chapter 8 concludes the book.

Do you know why you act, speak, or behave the way you do? Do you act, speak, and behave like that sometimes, or all the time? Do you know what determines your words and actions? What controls the way you speak, act and behave? In other words, do you know what you are full of?

Well, read on, and you will soon know!

CHAPTER TWO

Pregnancy

I am male by gender, but I can write about this subject with some 'authority', because, believe you me, I know what it means to be pregnant! How do I know? You might ask. Well, I have a husband (the Holy Spirit—Ha ha ha!), who has made me pregnant so many times. I carried many pregnancies to their full term, delivered well, never aborted or miscarried! In fact, this book is one of the pregnancies I carried till it was born. I have felt the 'discomfort', I have had to make the necessary 'adjustments' and I have felt the pain, especially at 'child birth'. I have also experienced the immediate release of relief and joy that comes with birth or delivery. You dig it?

If you think this sounds rather too spiritual, then let us go back to the physical. But before we do that, let me assert one point. I believe that whatever happens in the physical realm is a mirror, or a reflection, of what actually obtains in the Spiritual. For example, in the physical a man has to be born. In the Spiritual, a man has to be 'born again'. In both worlds, you cannot exist without being born! In the physical, a man[4] has to eat food in order to grow. Well, in the Spiritual, if you do not feed on the word of God you will not grow. Infact, in the physical, if you stop eating completely, you die. So it is in the Spiritual too—if you stop feeding on the Spiritual food, the Word of God, you die!—Spiritually. In the physical you clean yourself in many ways on a regular (if not daily!) basis. In the Spiritual, you need the Word of God (or the threshing floor) to rid yourself of all sorts and forms of 'dirt' that cling on you, otherwise you stink! I could go on and on. You get it? Well, this is what this book is all about. We discuss what happens in the physical realm, so we can draw parallels to what obtains in the Spiritual sphere. In the physical you get filled up with things—in the Spiritual you also get full of stuff—and in both spheres, the fundamental principle of this book holds true: Whatever fills you, controls you.

Now let us look at pregnancy. Let us start with a verse, shall we? The Bible says in **II Samuel 11:5:**

> 5 *And the woman conceived, and sent and told David, and said, I am with child.*

That's what happens when a woman conceives, right? It's a fancy way of saying it don't you think? 'I am with child'. She meant she was pregnant. Some people say 'I am expecting'. That's also another interesting way of putting it.

---

4 By 'man' here I mean as in reference to mankind. Gender-neutral sense. I certainly do not mean to be sexist, and I will never be! I use it in the context of John 3:1-5 and II Corinthians 5:17.

Check out what the Bible says in **Genesis 25:21-24:**

> 21 *And Isaac intreated the LORD for his wife, because she was barren: and the LORD was intreated of him, and Rebekah his wife conceived.*[22] *And the children struggled together within her; and she said, If it be so, why am I thus? And she went to enquire of the LORD.*[23] *And the LORD said unto her, Two nations are in thy womb, and two manner of people shall be separated from thy bowels; and the one people shall be stronger than the other people; and the elder shall serve the younger.*[24] *And when her days to be delivered were fulfilled, behold, there were twins in her womb.*

That's the story of two famous twins in the Bible: Esau and Jacob. Rebekkah, a mother of nations. She was pregnant, with twins. She must have been very full by the time she 'delivered'. **John 16:21** says:

> 21 *A woman when she is in travail hath sorrow, because her hour is come: but as soon as she is delivered of the child, she remembereth no more the anguish, for joy that a man is born into the world.*

Imagine how pregnancy affected Rebekkah's character, actions, attitude and behaviour in between. Imagine her anguish and pain at the critical moment of delivery. Why would she behave like that? Well, you know the answer now—What fills you, controls you. I can see you are getting excited—you can see where all this is going—or do you?

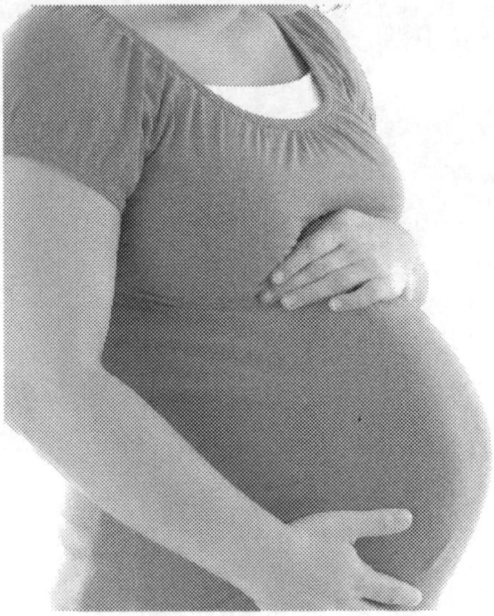

'With child'. Conceived. 'Expecting'. 'Pregnant'. '*Kumitiswa*[5]'. Whichever way you want to put it. It amounts to the same thing. In my vernacular language, they use another somewhat vulgar word, '*kuzadzwa*'(to be filled up), which kind of resonates with the theme of this book! A living organism has suddenly begun to develop inside the womb of a woman. Whether or not she is married is irrelevant for the purposes of this book. I shall leave the discussion of the psychological and sociological impact to the experts in those fields. I just concentrate on what everyone can see—the physiological. Something has entered her womb and begins to violate her space. Things are about to change! Physical gymnastics. The woman is technically filled up with the unborn child. Her womb is full, and continues to expand daily for nine months! It will be a case of the full getting fuller! And what did

[5] I am not sure what this word actually means, but its used in my vernacular language as some kind of 'slang', understood to refer to a woman impregnated by a man she is not married to.

I say? Whatever fills you, controls you. Well, let's analyse what happens.

I have had the privilege at least of watching my wife 'nurse' this thing called pregnancy from conception to delivery/birth. Like you, I have also observed other women during their times of pregnancy. Their behavioural traits are similar in many respects—so allow me to generalise. They will be full of the unborn child. Whatever fills you, controls you. Let us put this to the test.

Generally, when a woman gets pregnant, many things begin to change. For a start, some begin to spit quite a lot. Older mums are quick to tell if their teenage daughter has become 'secretly' pregnant . . . she will begin to 'spit-spit' all of a sudden. What fills you, controls you.

A pregnant woman will suddenly change their diet and eating habits. They begin to eat some strange stuff. My wife at one time started eating soil! She would send me on errands to get special soil from up the trees (a trail of soil particles used as a protective wall, built by termites). She was not only being controlled by what was inside her, she also became very controlling even of me! I was in trouble if I did not get her that soil! Oh my days! It wasn't funny! She also started eating raw mangoes—yes, that's right—the hard, unripe ones! She also started eating a whole bunch of other stuff she would not normally eat. What was going on? Well, now I guess you know the answer—thanks to this book. She was pregnant. She was full. Whatever fills you, controls you.

Have you not noticed that when a woman is pregnant or 'full' (*kuita kuzara!*), even her step changes. Her sleeping pattern changes. Adjustments galore! Her moods change. She suddenly begins to wear over-sized dresses etc. etc. Her dress code changes. I could go on and on. You know! A lot of things change[6]. There comes a time when she is eventually unable to bend over to pick anything she may drop. Somebody else has to do it for her. She is under some influential force. She is full of it. She cannot resist it. She has to obey whatever it commands her to do. She has lost control of herself—something else is in charge. Whatever fills you, controls you. True saying, that! And all the women say—'Amen!'

An interesting thing happened in the Bible, when two pregnant women met! **Luke 1:39-45** says:

> 39 *And Mary arose in those days, and went into the hill country with haste, into a city of Juda;*
> 40 *And entered into the house of Zacharias, and saluted Elisabeth.*
> 41 *And it came to pass, that, when Elisabeth heard the salutation of Mary, the babe leaped in her womb; and Elisabeth was filled with the Holy Ghost:*
> 42 *And she spake out with a loud voice, and said, Blessed art thou among women, and blessed is the fruit of thy womb.*
> 43 *And whence is this to me, that the mother of my Lord should come to me?*
> 44 *For, lo, as soon as the voice of thy salutation sounded in mine ears, the babe leaped*

---

6 You can think of other examples.

> *in my womb for joy.*[45] *And blessed is she that believed: for there shall be a performance of those things which were told her from the Lord.*

You wonder why a pregnant Mary would travel 'with haste' into a hill country. Did she go alone? Was Joseph with her? Well, we are not told, so we will never know. But what we know is that she went to the house of Zacharias. Apparently she did not speak to the man. She 'saluted Elisabeth'. The greeting caused an earthquake in the wombs of the two women. Apparently the foetuses communicated—somehow. Not really surprising, knowing that Mary was pregnant with Jesus our Lord, and Elizabeth with His forerunner, John. Now, a strange thing happened here. Elisabeth, already 'full' with the baby, got another kind of filling! She was 'filled with the Holy Ghost'. A double fill for Elisabeth. When the second filling took over, suddenly the quiet housewife began to make some noise. She 'spake out with a loud voice'. Surely, what fills you controls you. I am sure both Mary and Zacharias were surprised. The poor housewife of the priest began to prophesy! Ah! What's going on Elisabeth? She has been filled—again! This time with the Holy Ghost! You see . . . when that 'thing' called the Holy Ghost fills you, you kinda begin to act 'strange'. And so we see Elisabeth's sudden transformation—from a housewife to a prophet. Complete metamorphosis! Transformation. Transmutation. How did she know 'what' Mary was carrying? Notice she was the first to call the unborn baby 'my Lord'. Now, that's what I call revelation. She was filled with the Holy Spirit. Prophecy, pregnant woman!

It's a double-whammy for you. Prophecy! True to the thesis in this book . . . what fills you, controls you. She was suddenly Prophetess Elisabeth! Oh, how I would also like to be filled with that Holy Ghost stuff! Anyway, we shall return to this later. But eish! Yah!

Let me close this 'pregnancy' chapter with this passage of scripture in **Psalm 139:13-15**:

> 13 *For thou hast possessed my reins: thou hast covered me in my mother's womb.*
> 14 *I will praise thee; for I am fearfully and wonderfully made: marvellous are thy works; and that my soul knoweth right well.*
> 15 *My substance was not hid from thee, when I was made in secret, and curiously wrought in the lowest parts of the earth.*

While you were still in your mother's womb, God did an awesome thing. He 'fearfully' and 'wonderfully' made YOU. While your mother was full of you, God was busy making you 'in secret'. No matter who you are, no matter how tall, long or short you are; you are fearfully and wonderfully made! You are precious matter. You are beautiful, whatever size you are. You are precious material, made and fashioned by the master Himself. No matter what others say or think about you, remember you are 'fearfully and wonderfully made'. Be full of this knowledge, don't be filled with negative thoughts about yourself, or unhelpful comments of others. Remember, whatever fills you, controls you. Be filled with the knowledge that God took the trouble to make YOU, just as you are. Fearfully. Wonderfully. Made. By God! Ah, what more do you want? *Wozodei?*

Let us move on. Let us analyse the other things that fill people up. We discuss how those things end up influencing their actions, thoughts and behaviours.

CHAPTER THREE

Alcohol and Drugs

Beer, Wine and 'Spirits'

I have no idea who invented alcohol, but I think you will agree with me that it is one of the substances you find everywhere, and it is certainly one substance that has had an impact on society worldwide. Each society has its own traditional or local brew. Brewers use different raw materials and mechanisms, from the most basic to the modern, industrialized ways. Villagers in Africa have their own traditional brews, of different strengths. They use different materials, different tools, but funny enough, with the same effect on mankind—drink the stuff, and you are knocked out of our normal senses. In the developed world, production of alcoholic beverages has become a huge industry—and it continues to grow. Men at work—busy making stuff that knocks man out. Interesting!

There is another factor that I find fascinating about alcohol. Everybody agrees that it is a substance that does not have a positive effect on a human being—the one who takes it and the others around him/her. Yet those who take the stuff keep going back to it over and over again. It seems that once you start taking alcohol, it has such a grip on you that even if you want to stop you cannot. They call it addiction. They know it. They are the ones who gave it a name. Addiction. The more you take the stuff, the more you are hooked. Then they give you another nickname. They call you an Alcoholic! There are many who are busy taking care of people who have developed this disease. In the developed world it has become a business for some people. Many charity organizations are involved to try and help those under the invasive, abusive influence of alcohol[7]. Why people keep going back to it is what continues to intrigue me.

---

7 One that immediately comes to mind is called Alcoholics Anonymous. Also the Salvation Army church helps out a lot of the addicts at their premises worldwide, among many other organisations.

I have heard that some have promoted alcohol saying that they take the drink in order to 'drown their sorrows'. Ah, Nice one! Now, if that was true—and I believe many people believe this story to this day!—then I do not think that anybody would still be having any sorrows or problems in the world! If we understand the meaning of the word 'drown', then you get what I mean. If something drowns, it dies. It does not resurrect. So if you go down to the local (as they call it)—that's reference to the nearest pub—today, then you drink till you drop, but get home still alive—presumably all your sorrows will have been drowned that day. That should surely do you for the next year or two! You would surely need some time to gather more sorrows in your bag before you go back to drown them. It would then be a cycle. Perhaps then I would understand why people would occasionally take this sort of stuff. But hey—those who are on it cannot spend a single day without taking alcohol. Some even think they will die if they do not drink a pint or two. Yeah. That's why they call it an addiction.

Whether one drinks occasionally, or one has become an addict or an official alcoholic, my point in this book remains—once you are full of beer, wine or 'spirits', the stuff controls everything about you: the way you think, the way you speak, the way you act, and the way you behave. No-one can argue with this. You put the stuff inside you. It fills up your God-given system, then it messes it up. It takes you on, hook, line and sinker. It controls you; the whole of you. It invades your system. You are full of alcohol. Like a virus, it corrupts your system. So I say; Whatever fills you, controls you.

No doubt you will find it impossible to disagree with me on this. If you ever took this stuff before, check what you said, check what you did, check the way you behaved. You will most probably not be very proud of any of it. So you will perhaps begin to wonder like me—so what's the point?

If you have never taken alcohol before, good on you. But I am sure you have seen someone drunk before. You have seen the actions and behaviour or language of someone under the influence of drink. So you know what I am talking about—even from mere observation. It is a true saying: What fills you, controls you. Even the Bible has a number of examples of God's people who succumbed to the corrosive and destructive effect of alcoholic drinks. They took the stuff, with disastrous consequences. Let us look at a few examples.

Servants of God Under the Influence of Drink

Noah.

In **Gen. 9:19-27**, the Bible says:

> 19 *These are the three sons of Noah: and of them was the whole earth overspread.*
> 20 *And Noah began to be an husbandman, and he planted a vineyard:*
> 21 *And he drank of the wine, and was drunken; and he was uncovered within his tent.*
> 22 *And Ham, the father of Canaan, saw the nakedness of his father, and told his two brethren without.*
> 23 *And Shem and Japheth took a garment, and laid it upon both their shoulders, and went backward, and covered the nakedness of their father; and their faces were backward, and they saw not their father's nakedness.*
> 24 *And Noah awoke from his wine, and knew what his younger son had done unto him.*
> 25 *And he said, Cursed be Canaan; a servant of servants shall he be unto his brethren.*
> 26 *And he said, Blessed be the LORD God of Shem; and Canaan shall be his servant.*
> 27 *God shall enlarge Japheth, and he shall dwell in the tents of Shem; and Canaan shall be his servant.*

In the Bible, this is the first time we see the influence of alcohol on man. The man who took over from Abraham got drunk one day—yes, just one day! He filled himself with alcoholic wine. Stuff he presumably had made himself, or through his servants. What fills you, controls you. When Noah became full of wine, he lost control of his normal senses. He lost control of his dignity. The drink took over, and for reasons only best known to Noah himself (and of-course the wine!), the man decided to take his garments (or clothes) off. He stripped naked! I know there is lots of spiritual significance to the story too, but let's stick to the bare bones of the story for now. He was filled with alcoholic drink. The drink controlled his actions and behaviour. His poor son, Ham, was the first to see (perhaps for the first time ever) his father in his 'birthday suit' so to speak. Perhaps he should have been the first to cover his father (like the other sons did), but the poor young man was possibly too shocked—and he went and told his brothers. To this day, everybody salutes Shem and Japheth for their exemplary and spiritually significant response.

I have heard many preachers touch on this passage of scripture and they have said pretty much the same thing. When your father is exposed, a good child will do well to cover his nakedness. He/she would not tell even his/her brothers and sisters. Minimise the damage. Do not expose your father's weakness. Do not expose your father's nakedness. A good child will not run to tell the world. They just cover the father's nakedness, and God blesses them as a result. If the man of God has made a mistake, God does not allow others to judge or condemn him. He wants to deal with his servants Himself. So He says; 'Touch not my anointed ones' (**I Chron. 16:20-22; Ps. 105:13-15**[8]). It's a lesson the Church has learned, but it came after the servant of God succumbed to the influence of strong drink. Servants of God would therefore do

---

8 [13] *When they went from one nation to another, from one kingdom to another people;*[14] *He suffered no man to do them wrong: yea, he reproved kings for their sakes;*[15] *Saying, Touch not mine anointed, and do my prophets no harm.*

well to refrain from alcohol. Well, now you know why: what fills you, controls you.

Lot

The account of Lot's story is found in **Gen. 19:30-38**, which goes thus:

> [30] *And Lot went up out of Zoar, and dwelt in the mountain, and his two daughters with him; for he feared to dwell in Zoar: and he dwelt in a cave, he and his two daughters.*[31] *And the firstborn said unto the younger, Our father is old, and there is not a man in the earth to come in unto us after the manner of all the earth:*[32] *Come, let us make our father drink wine, and we will lie with him, that we may preserve seed of our father.*[33] *And they made their father drink wine that night: and the firstborn went in, and lay with her father; and he perceived not when she lay down, nor when she arose.*[34] *And it came to pass on the morrow, that the firstborn said unto the younger, Behold, I lay yesternight with my father: let us make him drink wine this night also; and go thou in, and lie with him, that we may preserve seed of our father.*[35] *And they made their father drink wine that night also: and the younger arose, and lay with him; and he perceived not when she lay down, nor when she arose.*[36] *Thus were both the daughters of Lot with child by their father.*[37] *And the firstborn bare a son, and called his name Moab: the same is the father of the Moabites unto this day.*[38] *And the younger, she also bare a son, and called his name Benammi: the same is the father of the children of Ammon unto this day.*

Watch what happened here. A man, an adult, got so drunk that he absolutely had no idea what was happening around him! He was completely knocked out for seven by the wine! Wow! Read verse 33 again. The first daughter came in. He didn't even notice. She did whatever she did, however she did it, still the man felt nothing! Or rather, he was too drunk—or too full—to realise what was going on. Somebody came and completely violated his private space, went away, and he did not realise. He woke up the next morning, still had no idea what happened the night before! I guess he was still drunk! Is that not what they call hangover?

Funny enough, those who make money from alcohol are very smart. They say the only way to cure 'hangover' is to take more alcohol! Is that daft or what?? Surely!? It's like a preacher who says: 'the only way to stop sinning is to sin some more!'

Yet Jesus Christ gave the opposite message to the woman who was caught in adultery. Read the story in **John 8:3-11**. As the woman's accusers disappeared with their tails in between their legs, the matter concludes by saying (verse 10-11):

> 10*When Jesus had lifted up himself, and saw none but the woman, he said unto her, Woman, where are those thine accusers? hath no man condemned thee?* 11 *She said, No man, Lord. And Jesus said unto her, Neither do I condemn thee: go, and sin no more."*

Well, I wish someone had said to Lot; 'Go, and drink no more'. But, alas, there was no one to give him such a message. The girls continued with their mission. I think they must have known about what I am saying here—what fills you controls you.

So the story goes on. The next day, while Lot was still under the stupor of last night's drama, they added insult to injury. I guess he was now too drunk even to say 'No'. So they made him take in more of the stuff. He was knocked out. Completely. *Kuita kuzara*! The second girl went and did her thing. Sordid stuff—when you think about it. Hey, the man was totally incapacitated! I wonder how they managed to do it. Well, that's besides the point. At least this story really drives my point home. People get so drunk that they absolutely have no control over their own body! No awareness whatsoever of goings on around them! Not even an ability to recall (or remember) anything the next day! Now, that's serious, guys! You can get so drunk that someone can chop your hand off and you have no idea who did it or when, where or how it happened! *Maiwee!*

I now remember a late brother of mine who was so hooked on alcohol. He used to enjoy fights when drunk. So many times he would come home with all sorts of wounds but if you asked him he had no idea who inflicted them on him! People feared him whenever he was under the influence. Yet when he was not drunk, he was a most intelligent, most loving and caring man! When he was drunk, he did not care who he beat up, parents and all. The beer had this profound effect on him. Funny enough, he used to like beating up his wife when he got home. I used to live with them as a school-going young man. I remember one day at night, my sister in law got so angry she decided to revenge. After beating her up and causing the usual chaos in the house, he sat down and demanded that she give him his meal. As usual, my sister in law obliged, although she was upset. My brother sat on his favourite chair. Within a few minutes, he was fast asleep! He was snoring. He was so knocked out by the beer that after a while he started wetting himself while he sat.

My sister in law grabbed the moment for some revenge. She went into the kitchen, brought the wooden stick she would use to cook maize meal (sadza) with. I watched her beat him up on his legs with it. You could see that she was still in fear as she did it gently, and she was still doing it in love. The strikes were firm, but not harsh. At one time he wriggled and groaned—as if feeling the pain. He never woke up, though! She tried to lift him up to take him to the bedroom (may her soul rest in peace!), but he was too knocked out and so very difficult to carry. I tried to help her but we failed. Reluctantly she left him to spend the night there.

The next morning he was lying on the floor. When he got up he was saying that he felt pain in his legs, but he was 'fine'. He had no idea how he got the pain. As usual, he washed up, had his breakfast (maize meal with vegetables and some meat) and away he went to work! Ah! Alcohol really knocks people out. I saw it with my own eyes. Perhaps my brother was not as drunk as Lot that night, but hey—the man was totally out. Completely paralysed by alcohol.

What more can I say? Men and women, boys and girls, servants of God—please do us a favour—don't get stuffed with this stuff! Abstain. Stay away. Remain sober—and remain YOURSELF!

Other Biblical Passages of Scripture

The Bible is also full of references to the subject of alcohol. Many are said to have set aside good judgement due to the influence of drink.

Check out for **example Proverbs 20:1; 23:29-35; 31:2-9; Isaiah 5:21-23; 56:9-12; Hosea 4:11-12.**

Ephesians 5:18 says:

> *18. And be not drunk with wine, wherein is excess; but be filled with the Spirit;*

Here, being drunk with wine is compared and contrasted with being "filled with the Spirit." I shall come back to this same scripture later on in the book, when we talk about the effect of being filled with the Holy Spirit. Although the results of these two influences are very different, the principle remains the same—what fills you, controls you.

The thing that interests me here is the word 'spirit' with reference to alcohol. Have you noticed that those alcoholic drinks with greater alcohol content are referred to as 'spirits'. I mean, the 'strong stuff' as others call it. Even in restaurants, there is a 'Wine and Spirits' section on the menu. Indeed, the devil is a master copy-cat! He surely knows the principle—what fills you controls you. He surely must have studied what people do when they are filled with the Holy Spirit (for instance, they become generous and give a lot to the Church and other worthy, charitable causes). So he devised a plan. He says something like this: You don't have to go to Church to be filled with the Spirit—just go to the pub instead! Get the 'Spirits' there, they are sure to fill you up. And once they have filled you up, they take complete control over you! Smart, eh! Well, not to me!

Ah! Who is fooling who? I would rather be filled with the Holy Spirit, than with the alcoholic 'spirits' which cause men and women to forget about themselves, and neglect their families. Some people who like their drink completely disregard their families. They 'blow' away all the money on booze and other related 'luxuries' at the expense of their spouses and children. Funny enough, when the same person comes to church, they won't even put a penny in the offering basket—complaining that the Church likes money too much. They complain about tithes and offerings in the church (which together amount to just over ten percent of their earnings), yet when they 'go out' they blow away in one weekend a whole lot MORE than a Christian would spend at Church in a month!

A man walks to a pub, spends quite a lot, when drunk he takes a taxi or cab home (which is a few minutes away), but the cab or taxi driver goes around the block before bringing the drunk man home—to make more money! If the drunken man makes the mistake of driving home—ignoring Government's advice which says 'Do not drink and drive'—first of all he will stagger to the vehicle, and very soon the vehicle will be staggering too—with disastrous consequences to the driver and other innocent, sober road users! Better be late, than be the late!

For the drunk who is wise enough to take a ride or a taxi home, watch what happens when the taxi gets to his address. For a fare charge of say £5.00, the drunkard gets £20.00 out of his pocket or wallet (funny how he remembers where his wallet is!), and waves good bye to the driver—saying 'Keep change!' as he staggers into his house! Ask the same man for a pound (£1) tomorrow, and he won't budge! You see, when you are drunk, you live a life without self-control (itself part of the fruit of the Spirit—see **Galatians 5:16-23, II Timothy 1:7**), you live under the control of the alcohol, and of dangerous, evil impulses and desires. You dig it? Surely, what fills you, controls you. Don't be filled with wine! Don't fill yourself with 'wine and spirits'. Rather be filled with the Holy Spirit. Don't be full of alcohol! If you have to drink, drink water instead! You get healthier as a result!

Although I do not want to belabor the point, let us look at a few more passages of scripture.

In **1 Corinthians 11:17-34**, you find that those who were given to much drinking even led the Church to a shameful celebration of the Lord's death, and resulted in judgment. Drunkenness causes people to lose control of themselves and to do things they should not, that is why Christians are commanded to present their bodies to God as instruments of righteousness (see **Rom. 6**). Even though they may have been drunkards before, Christians are exhorted not to live in drunkenness as they once did (**1 Peter 4:1-5**). Children of God are expected to bring their bodies under control, and not to be controlled by bodily appetites (**1 Corinthians 9:24-27**). Paul, the Apostle of Jesus Christ advises the Christian to learn from the failures of the ancient Israelites (**1 Corinthians 10:1-13**), who gave in to their appetites.

Proverbs 20:1 says:

> *Wine [is] a mocker, strong drink [is] raging: and whosoever is deceived thereby is not wise.*

See what wine does? It makes you a mocker. Strong drink makes you a raging animal. Well, be wise child of God. Avoid both.

Check out what the Bible says in **Proverbs 23:29-35**!

> 29 *Who hath woe? who hath sorrow? who hath*
> *contentions? who hath babbling? who hath wounds*
> *without cause? who hath redness of eyes?* 30 *They that*
> *tarry long at the wine; they that go to seek mixed*
> *wine.* 31 *Look not thou upon the wine when it is red,*
> *when it giveth his colour in the cup, [when] it moveth*
> *itself aright.* 32 *At the last it biteth like a serpent, and*
> *stingeth like an adder.* 33 *Thine eyes shall behold strange*
> *women, and thine heart shall utter perverse things.* 34
> *Yea, thou shalt be as he that lieth down in the midst*

> *of the sea, or as he that lieth upon the top of a mast.*[35] *They have stricken me, [shalt thou say, and] I was not sick; they have beaten me, [and] I felt [it] not: when shall I awake? I will seek it yet again.*

Look at the effect of being filled with alcohol and strong drink. See verse 29. You will have 'woe'. Oh, I don't like this word. It's a very small word, but every time it is used in the Bible, it spells disaster. Go check it out yourself. You will be filled with 'sorrow'. You will have 'contentions'—that's strife, arguments, disagreements, violent disputes. Ah, who wants any of those? You will have 'babbling'—that's jabbering, unhelpful, senseless talk. Mama lo! You will have 'wounds without cause'. As we have already discussed, you get injured, and you won't even know how you got the wounds! You get injured for nothing. *Unokuvara*! Look, it goes on to say you will have 'redness of eyes'. Ever seen a drunkard? Why have red eyes? All this packed in just one little verse! Verse 30 tells you why. Surely, what fills you controls you.

If you fill yourself with strong drink, check its further effects in verse 32. It bites like a serpent. It stings like an adder. Have you ever experienced a snake bite? You might take it for granted if you have never had one. Most people died as a result of snake bites. Some survived, but with serious deformities. Taking alcohol is being likened to having a snake bite. Think about it. *Pafunge*! When you are full of alcohol, your eyes see and get attracted to people that mess up your family relationships, and your relationship with the Lord. Further, you utter all sorts of perversion. You stubbornly and stupidly say and do unreasonable, irrational, unwise things. You end up living in regret.

Oh, it gets worse! See verse 34 and 35. You even think it's wise to use the sea as your bed! Of-course if you do that you drown! That's worse than foolish. You will try the impossible—laying on top of a mast. Oh my God! You think it wise to lay on top of a pole! You know what will happen, right? The pole will simply make a huge hole through you! If you are lucky and it misses you, you will obviously fall to the ground—and you may either get seriously injured, or you may die! Hey! Do you see this? Taking alcohol is like doing all these things. Ah! I sit!

The last verse confirms what we said earlier. You get things done to you, but you are so knocked out you have no idea what goes on around you, like Lot. You get up the next morning. You take heed of the enemy's usual advice: to get rid of the beer, go drink some more! That's the snare of alcohol—the devil's big bait. And so you decide: 'I will seek it yet again'. So the cycle continues. The devil wants you hooked forever. He wants you to remain drunk till Jesus Christ appears in the clouds—and you won't even notice! No doubt you will notice when you wake up in hell—because God made sure there is none of it there—only a pit full of hell fire! Oh, I don't wish for anyone to go there! So please, please, do yourself a favour. Refrain. Run away from beer and other strong alcoholic drinks. Live, and let live!

For those in leadership at any level, the Bible says in **Proverbs 31: 4-5**:

> 4 *It is not for kings, O Lemuel, it is not for kings to drink wine; nor for princes strong drink:*
> 5 *Lest they*

> *drink, and forget the law, and pervert the judgment of any of the afflicted.*

Well, I think this is straightforward enough. What fills you controls you. Leaders do well to avoid alcohol, lest they pervert the judgement on people! Who needs a drunk leader?

Prophet Isaiah says (**Is. 5:11**)[9]:

> 11 *Woe unto them that rise up early in the morning, [that] they may follow strong drink; that continue until night, [till] wine inflame them!*

Oh, that small word again! Woe. Woe unto them that even rise early in the morning looking for stuff that keeps them hooked. The drink inflames them. You know what flames do? You burn—alive! Well, need I say more?

Again, the blessed prophet says in **Isaiah 28: 1, 7-8**:

> 1 *Woe to the crown of pride, to the drunkards of Ephraim, whose glorious beauty is a fading flower, which are on the head of the fat valleys of them that are overcome with wine! . . .* 7 *But they also have erred through wine, and through strong drink are out of the way; the priest and the prophet have erred through strong drink, they are swallowed up of wine, they are out of the way through strong drink; they err in vision,*

---

9 Also read Is. 19:14 which says: 14 *The LORD hath mingled a perverse spirit in the midst thereof: and they have caused Egypt to err in every work thereof, as a drunken man staggereth in his vomit.*

> *they stumble in judgment.*[8] *For all tables are full of vomit and filthiness, so that there is no place clean.*

That little word again! Woe! See what happens when priests and prophets fill themselves with this sort of stuff instead of being filled with the Holy Spirit! Just imagine! They err through wine. They get out of the way. They get swallowed up by the wine or strong drink. They err in vision. That means they begin to lead people the wrong way—astray! Indeed, what fills you controls you. They are unable to make sound judgements. Look!—Even the pulpits and tables in the Church of God become full of vomit! Oh, my; Oh my! Horrible, smelly stuff coming out of prophets and priests! *Maiwee!!* It gets so bad people can't even clean up!

See the instruction God gave to Aaron, the first High Priest, the first Archbishop, in **Leviticus 10:8-11:**

> [8] *And the LORD spake unto Aaron, saying,*[9] *Do not drink wine nor strong drink, thou, nor thy sons with thee, when ye go into the tabernacle of the congregation, lest ye die: [it shall be] a statute for ever throughout your generations:*[10] *And that ye may put difference between holy and unholy, and between unclean and clean;*[11] *And that ye may teach the children of Israel all the statutes which the LORD hath spoken unto them by the hand of Moses.*

This instruction reinforces all I am saying in this book. Oh, servants of God, Refrain! Avoid alcohol completely. Do the children of God a favour. Don't touch!

'POVO Inoguta!'

Over the years, I have witnessed all sorts of sordid behaviour perpetrated by different people who were filled with strong drink. I am sure you also have had some similar experiences, one way or the other. Let me give you one of my 'favourite' examples. This involves part of my own family. I like to give my own family's examples for obvious reasons—without mentioning names of-course[10].

I have an uncle who used to drink traditional beer with his wife. Both man and wife liked the cup. It was in the village setting. One weekend both husband and wife went drinking with others at some homestead. Traditional, strong beer which they nicknamed 'Seven Days'—because it took seven days to prepare before it would be ready for consumption. Others would prepare the stronger stuff, nicknamed '*kachasu*'. Nobody ever told me what this means—but I was made to understand that it was the version of 'spirits' or the strong stuff—prepared traditional style. African Science, origin, Malawi. People in our villages knew how to prepare this stuff. You drink it, and it knocks you out! Whether my uncle and his wife took that stuff that weekend, in addition to the 'Seven Days', I do not know.

---

[10] Most examples I use are things that actually happened in the past. However, most of my family have since converted to Christ. So the stories are now like part of one's 'testimony'. See what the Lord can do! See how far we have come! Jesus is Lord!

I was out there playing with other young people of the village, while the adults did their thing of drinking. I remember we were playing some kind of 'football'—a piece of cloth wrapped around by a rope in a plastic bag. Then suddenly we were surprised by a lot of noise coming from the adults. People were shouting and screaming. Others were sort of running away from the scene in apparent 'shame'. Apparently my uncle and his wife had had an argument. It then exploded into a huge farce. As curious young people, we rushed to the scene. My aunt was very angry. Lo and behold! My aunt had taken off her top, her blouse. She was fuming, shouting and cursing. Suddenly there was a huge circle of men and women, boys and girls around her. She was in the middle—furious, pacing about—chanting and ranting. Then—all of a sudden my aunt shocked the crowd. She began to lift her skirt all the way to her hips—shouting and singing gleefully. She was saying:

> *"Povo Inoguta! Povo ngaigute! Povo ichaguta, ichiona, ichifara!"*
>
> *"Povo Inoguta! Povo ngaigute! Povo ichaguta, ichiona, ichifara!"*[11]

---

[11] A literal translation would be something like: 'The public (povo) shall be full/fed (as in having taken enough food)! Let the public be fed! The public shall be fed, they shall see, and they shall enjoy! Let the public be fed. Let them see. Let them enjoy!' The word 'povo' is a word used to refer to ordinary people as opposed to the leaders. It was a commonly used word in Zimbabwe before, during and after the liberation struggle—the struggle for Zimbabwean independence. My aunt ended up having a nickname based on her song. People started calling her VaPovo Inoguta (Madam Public Shall Be Fed).

She went on and on. Every time she got to the end of her song, she would open her skirt wide, then her legs too. She did this quite a few times before some women restrained her and took her away. She wanted to fix her husband by displaying what she called 'his things' to the public. Apparently she did not have a pant or knickers on. As a young and innocent boy, that day I saw things I had never seen. My aunt was full of alcohol. Filled with traditional beer. The stuff took total control of her behaviour that day. It was totally out of character. She shocked the community (and of-course shamed her husband and us her family) by what she did that day. Funny enough (well, perhaps it's not funny anymore) she could not remember a thing when we asked her the next morning. She could not believe what everybody was saying! Wow! What more can I say? It is really a true saying: What fills you, controls you. Please don't get drunk, lest you behave like my aunt one day. Ah, *Povo inoguta*? Oh, Noo!

Expensive Urine

If you ever went into a restaurant anywhere in the world, you will probably have discovered what I found. The prices on the section called 'Wine and Spirits' are very high. The stronger the alcohol content, the more expensive the drink! Most of the drinks there will be more expensive than the food! The same holds true if you go to the pub, or the bottle store or supermarket to buy beer and other alcoholic drinks.

Everyone who takes alcohol, beer and related strong drinks like vodka, whisky, brandy, gin, applejack, tequila, baijiu, port, sherry, madeira, etc will agree that there is very little benefit apart from socialising and getting drunk[12]. I am not sure if the resultant pot-belly is one of the expected benefits! Liquor has debatably very little nutritional value to the human body, yet this stuff is so expensive! Here is another very interesting thing. When you are full of this stuff, you make numerous trips to the toilet. That means you take the liquor in, it releases its venom into your veins, muscles, tissues, ligaments, bones and bone marrow. Then you go and throw all that expensive liquid away. You go back and consume some more, chatting or whatever—with your mates. You fill up again and again, it releases its stuff inside of you, then you keep throwing away the liquid. And so the cycle goes on and on throughout the day. You have not gained much. Your body has

12 See http://en.wikipedia.org/wiki/Alcoholic_beverage

not gained much, yet you have spent lots of hard-earned money. All you will have done all day is to create expensive urine! That's my verdict. Expensive urine! Well, whether cheap or not—urine is urine. It smells, it collects germs and all sorts of unhealthy things. Have you not seen how drunkards sometimes don't even go to the toilet? And even if they do go, have you not seen them missing that big whatever—which is meant to receive the urine and safely deposit it away? The result? The toilet stinks. The environment suffers. Our children get unhealthier. They get weaker. Some even die due to a germ-infested environment. Families pick up the bills for correctional medicines. Government and the NHS[13] step in at the taxpayer's expense. Ah! Expensive Urine!

Celebrities Behaving Badly—Fatal Combination of Drink and Drugs.

Surely alcohol is no respector of persons! No matter who you are, what class you belong to in society, the effect of beer/liquor and other strong drink is the same on people. It gets worse when people combine liquor with drugs. *Maiwee.* The lethal combination of liquor/alcohol and drugs is another leveller. Kings and paupers, presidents and citizens, rich and poor, educated and uneducated, 'black or white'[14], male or female, young or old: their effect or impact is the same. When full of this stuff, people act and behave

---

13 National Health Service in the United Kingdom.

14 I don't like this distinction. I regard it as derogatory and prejudicial—but I use it here only because that's unfortunately what most people are familiar with.

in the strangest of ways, way out of character. They become abnormal, or perhaps subnormal. I am sure you can think of many examples of people right across the spectrum of life—world leaders, celebrities, and other public figures (of-course including ordinary citizens) who succumbed to the powerful and corrosive influence of alcohol and drugs.

Consider, for example, certain celebrities in the music industry, both male and female, who had stories published in national and international newspapers and world-class magazines, whose stories were 'breaking news' on many a national news channel. Celebrities who failed to continue with their lucrative careers because of their love for the strong drink and other stuff that distorts the mind of man. How many of them come to mind. Intelligent, talented people who suffered the demise of alcohol and drugs, and had their careers—and lives—cut short. Painfully short. Beer and drugs. Terrible twins. Their casualties are many. Lots of young 'followers' or 'fans' who looked up to the celebrities in many ways—many of whom ended up following or copying their bad habits. They think it's 'cool'. Well, I believe that if any of those who passed on due to the influence of such addictive substances were to resurrect, they would advise all their 'fans' never to touch the stuff again! Unfortunately, most mortals only live once!

Add to this the sad stories of many sports stars, celebrities in the movies, 'powerful' politicians and world leaders who failed to lead or to govern due to the influence of alcohol and/or drugs. Some died as a direct consequence of taking these twin substances. Why? For what? Oh, how I wish all people of all walks of life would read this book and take heed of its warning and simple piece of advice. If you allow anything to fill you up, it will and shall control you. Choose with wisdom the things that you allow to fill you up. I would suggest you do not let alcohol and drugs be among them. Our world will fare better, if our celebrities and world leaders refrained from taking this deadly stuff. If they have to drink, why not drink fruit juice, water or other non-alcoholic beverages—of which there are plenty on the market! Through this book I urge all citizens of the world, irrespective of class, race, colour, wealth, education or whatever, to shun these deadly substances. Surely our world will get better as a result. Celebrities. Leaders. Public figures. Ordinary folk. Young and old. Male and female. Are you one of them? Well, remember: what fills you, controls you!

CHAPTER FOUR

Bitterness and Anger

These are terrible twins affecting human behaviour across the globe. These have a habit of 'rising up' like acid or yeast. Bitterness and anger surge from within the gut of a human being, until they are full. Suddenly they lash out. When filled with bitterness and anger, they come out like a tornado or hurricane. Some will behave like a twister or a tsunami. They destroy everything in their path, with so much ferocity and power. They will be filled. Driven to destruction by bitterness and anger. Indeed, it is true: whatever fills you, controls you.

Many strikes and other violent protests stem from this. I have seen images in newspapers, on television screens, in magazines and other forms of media. Images of people with mouths wide open, shouting all sorts of vile language at whoever is the subject or object of their anger. Like you, I have seen people arming themselves with bricks, stones, knobkerries and other sorts of 'missiles'—going about doing extensive and expensive damage to public buildings, public infrastructures such as electricity cables, bridges etc just to vent out their anger. Some call them strikes. Others call them (violent) protests. Yet others call them uprisings or revolutions. Whatever you may call them, they are public displays of the effect of being filled with bitterness and anger. The consequences are usually far-reaching, the clean-ups usually very costly.

Well, what can man do? Oh, how I wish we could all be a bit more long-suffering, more gentle, more loving and more forgiving. I wish we were all to receive and benefit from the fruit of the Spirit to guide our thoughts and behaviour—to govern our response mechanisms.

The Bible says in **Gal. 5:22-23**:

> 22 *But the fruit of the Spirit is love, joy, peace, longsuffering, gentleness, goodness, faith,*
> 23 *Meekness, temperance: against such there is no law.*

In other words, if everyone in the community were to respond to any situation under the guidance and influence of the Spirit of God (we shall return to this later on in the book), I am sure we would have significantly less of violence in our community and less of violent outbursts in our homes.

Watch out when a husband, father or mother is full of bitterness and anger. I have seen some angry women throw glasses and all sorts of cutlery at their spouses or 'loved ones'. Its funny how someone would go to town and buy a very expensive wide-screen flat television, then one day in a fit of rage and anger, they pick it up and smash it onto the floor—breaking it into shrapnel and tiny little pieces—well beyond repair. When all the bitterness and anger is gone later on, they begin to miss their TV, and the next day they go and buy another one—using a credit card! Ah, you are laughing!

The Cricket's Hind Legs (*Makumbo eGurwe*)

Ever heard of a cricket? Well, for your information, it is 'a leaping, chirping insect that has biting mouthparts, long legs, and antennae. The male produces a chirping sound by rubbing its forewings together'[15]. We had lots of these in the African village where I was born. In fact, we used to dig them up for meat. Yes, I grew up eating that sort of stuff. Imagine! I think it's still a delicacy back in my roots. Well, this book is not about food. So, let's get straight to my point.

As a young boy growing up and catching lots of crickets for food, one thing I observed was the violent nature of the cricket's reaction or response to capture. Understandably, no-one wants to be captured. No-one wants to be dug up for meat. Fair point, that. But hey, the cricket was special, especially the male ones. They had vicious, spiky hind legs. Their kick was very painful. But what I observed was that in anger, the cricket would so violently lash out with both of its hind legs—it would do it with so much force that

[15] Encarta Dictionary: English (U.K)

it would end up dislodging and throwing either one or both of its legs away. It would kick so bad that it would end up losing its own hind leg or legs in the process! So I would then think—what if I wanted to release this cricket back into the wild? It would go back totally disabled, wounded so badly that, unable to move, it would suffer a very painful death at the 'hands' of termites, ants and other predatory insects! I did that one day and released the cricket—without its hind legs. I went back the next day to the spot and found it exactly where I had left it—but fully covered with all sorts of ants and insects. They were feasting on it. I bet they were very grateful to me when they saw me—because none of them went away. Christmas had come early.

So, what's the point of this rather sad story? Well, it taught me a big lesson. So many people, when they get angry, their response is such that their actions are tantamount to losing one or both of their legs. Like the woman who smashed her own television in anger, such people kick out so violently that they sort of lose their own legs. They mess themselves up in the process—big time! They forget that they will need to walk again tomorrow! They permanently and fatally damage key people in their lives who they normally depend on—people who are like 'hind legs' in their lives. We all have our 'hind legs' people. Don't destroy your relationship with them in a fit of anger which comes like a twister. Don't do it. Avoid anger and bitterness. I have often heard people saying, 'Oh, I just lost it!' Well, I say don't lose it. You might never be able to pick it up again! Don't behave like the cricket. You will regret! Refuse to be filled with bitterness and anger. By responding in anger, you gain nothing and you lose much! Take heed!

Consider what the Bible says in **Hebrews 12:14-15:**

> *14.Follow peace with all men, and holiness, without which no man shall see the Lord: 15.Looking diligently lest any man fail of the grace of God; lest any root of bitterness springing up trouble you, and thereby many be defiled;*

See what bitterness does? When its root springs up, it creates trouble for you, and in the wake of your angry and destructive response, many are defiled! Instead of bitterness and anger, be filled with peace instead.

Ecclesiastes 7:9 admonishes:

> *9. Be not hasty in thy spirit to be angry: for anger resteth in the bosom of fools.*

Is this scripture harsh? I think not. Indeed, anger makes people speak and behave like fools, sometimes worse than fools. When you explode in anger, many people (including some innocent ones) will get hurt in the process. Many get affected. The Church suffers. The family suffers. Society suffers. You see, nobody benefits . . . not even the one who is angry! No wonder the wise man Solomon says 'anger rests in the bosom of fools.' Yes, fools. Don't you be one of them! And please do not make us to be fools! Refuse to be filled with the evil spirit of anger. Pray bitterness away, out of your bosom. Ask God to create in you a clean heart, and to renew a right spirit within you (see **Psalm 51: 10**). Yes, right spirit. That's what we all need. A sweet spirit. Oh Lord God, help us!

CHAPTER FIVE

Jealousy and Hatred

I would urge all God's children to forcefully reject the spirit of jealousy and hatred. These two terrible twins usually can lead to another terrible set of twins, namely witchcraft (physical and/or spiritual), and murder (physical and/or spiritual). If you allow them to fill you up, they drive you to malicious and murderous actions.

Filled with the spirit of Cain (Cain and Abel)

The first recorded murder story in the Bible was perpetrated by a brother who was driven to kill by the spirit of jealousy. It is the story of Cain and Abel, found in **Genesis 4:3-10**:

[3] *And in process of time it came to pass, that Cain brought of the fruit of the ground an offering unto the LORD.*[4] *And Abel, he also brought of the firstlings of his flock and of the fat thereof. And the LORD had respect unto Abel and to his offering:*[5] *But unto Cain and to his offering he had not respect. And Cain was very wroth, and his countenance fell.*[6] *And the LORD said unto Cain, Why art thou wroth? and why is thy countenance fallen?*[7] *If thou doest well, shalt thou not be accepted? and if thou doest not well, sin lieth at the door. And unto thee shall be his desire, and thou shalt rule over him.*[8] *And Cain talked with Abel his brother: and it came to pass, when they were in the field, that Cain rose up against Abel his brother, and slew him.*[9]*And the LORD said unto Cain, Where is Abel thy brother? And he said, I know not: Am I my brother's keeper?* [10]*And he said, What hast thou done? the voice of thy brother's blood crieth unto me from the ground.*

The two brothers offered different sacrifices to the LORD, and for reasons best known to God (there are different theological explanations on these 'offerings'), God found Abel's offering acceptable, and Cain's one was not. That drove Cain to jealousy. He allowed the spirit of jealousy to fill him. It brought with it its sister called hatred. Cain was full of jealousy and hatred. He was swelling inside. *Kuita kuzvimba*! Before he knew it, that which filled him controlled him, with fatal consequences. Just like that, while they were in conversation as brothers, 'Cain rose up against Abel his brother, and slew him'. Ouch! Ouch! Ouch!!

Children of God should not allow these terrible twins to enter them. They lead to murderous actions. Christians at each other's throat! No. No. No. That is not as it should be! Every time one Christian kills or maims (physically or spiritually) another under the motivation of jealousy, anger or hatred, I feel they should hear

God asking the same question—"Where is your brother/sister?" How many casualties do you have? If the number is greater than zero, you need to pray away the spirit of Cain, in the mighty name of Jesus Christ! To this day, God is still asking the question to those who maim and kill others: 'Where is your brother?' 'Where is your sister?' How do you respond? Like Cain? I pray not! You do not want to hear God asking you the second question: 'What have you done?' Indeed, you are your brother's keeper. Brothers and sisters should take care of each other. That's the way Christians should be. Refuse to be filled with the Cain spirit. Say 'No'. Say 'Amen'.

Murder plot after a father's funeral—Esau and Jacob

Check out the story of yet another two brothers, Esau and Jacob. Again, Esau was filled with jealousy, and the sister of jealousy—hatred—came to top it up. Then Esau was overflowing. *Kuita chidhafudhafu negodo*! Full of hatred—triggered by jealousy. *Sidhudhla*! Ah, *kuita kuzara*! Now, watch the strong words about Esau in **Genesis 27:41**;

> 41*And Esau hated Jacob because of the blessing wherewith his father blessed him: and Esau said in his heart, The days of mourning for my father are at hand; then will I slay my brother Jacob.*

Look again at the 'thing' that drives Christians to murder: jealousy. Jealousy begets hatred. Hatred begets anger. Anger begets murder. How I pray that every Christian would vigorously reject this spirit whenever it enters one's heart, no matter which form or shape it takes. The Bible tells us to resist the devil, and he will flee from us (**James 4:7**). You have to resist. You see, resistance is not passive. It should not be accommodating any sense of 'justification'. Brothers and sisters, we should not have any murderers in the body of Christ. I have come to realise that the Christian army is the only army where the combatants shoot their own wounded, or their own wounded comrades. More often than not, 'the Church' tends to finish off anyone known to have suffered injury through sin or failure of some sort. It is certainly not 'friendly fire'. He who has compassion does not pour water on a drowning mouse! There are some murderers in the Church at times.

Take a minute and read **1 John 3:11-15; and Gal. 5:14-15**. Think deeply about what the Word of God says in the scriptures you just read. The murderers referred to here are not out in the streets. They do not prowl about in the dark, waiting to kill unsuspecting travellers. The police are not looking for them. They wear nice clothes. Some of them even drive expensive cars. They live in nice houses, have comfortable lives. They carry a bible to Church every Sunday. Some of them are in the leadership of the Church. Murderers. Killers in suits and decent outfits. Murderers in the Church. Brothers and sisters, this is not as it should be. You now know what I am saying. What fills you controls you. Don't let this stuff fill you. Please!

Jealousy and Hatred: The plight of Joseph

I encourage you to read and consider the story of the plight of Joseph at the hands of his jealous brothers in **Genesis 37**. For purposes of space, I am not going to quote it here for you. Please, don't be lazy. Pose for a moment as you read this book. Read your Bible now. Read the story again, even if you know it. It's good to read. A group of brothers united by jealousy. Wow! What kind of unity is that? It amazes me how people who are evil tend to be more united than those who are not. Please pray that the twin spirits of jealousy and hatred do not befriend you. As I said before, jealousy breeds hatred, which in turn breeds murder. No wonder **1 John 2:9-11** says:

> [9]*He that saith he is in the light, and hateth his brother,*
> *is in darkness even until now.* [10]*He that loveth his*

> *brother abideth in the light, and there is none occasion of stumbling in him.* [11]*But he that hateth his brother is in darkness, and walketh in darkness, and knoweth not whither he goeth, because that darkness hath blinded his eyes.*

Similarly, **1 John 3:15** concludes:

> [15]*Whosoever hateth his brother is a murderer: and ye know that no murderer hath eternal life abiding in him.*

I consider these scriptures to be self-explanatory. I therefore urge all children of God to vigorously reject the spirit of jealousy. Envy. Do not covet. Learn to appreciate others who may have succeeded where you did not. Some people never try to do anything, yet become very jealous of those who try different things and succeed in some of them. Watch out for the sister-spirit of competition. Unhealthy competition breeds jealousy and resentment. Learn to be content with what you have got, what you have yourself achieved. We cannot all be the same. It's ok to be challenged and inspired by someone else's success, and then aspire to do the same in your own different way. But it's fatal to degenerate into the feelings of envy and jealousy. Fight this horrible spirit. Jealousy. Kick it out away every time it tries to visit you. Jealousy leads to witchcraft and murder. Ah, witchcraft! Hey—murder! Oh my God! Refuse to give room to spiritual witchcraft and wizardry. If you let these fill you, we perish! You know the reason—what fills you, controls you.

Put Off; Put On

Let us analyse what the Bible says in **Col. 3: 8-15**:

> 8 *But now ye also put off all these; anger, wrath, malice,*
> *blasphemy, filthy communication out of your mouth.* 9
> *Lie not one to another, seeing that ye have put off the*
> *old man with his deeds;* 10 *And have put on the new*
> *man, which is renewed in knowledge after the image*
> *of him that created him:* 11 *Where there is neither*
> *Greek nor Jew, circumcision nor uncircumcision,*
> *Barbarian, Scythian, bond nor free: but Christ is all,*
> *and in all.* 12 *Put on therefore, as the elect of God, holy*
> *and beloved, bowels of mercies, kindness, humbleness*
> *of mind, meekness, longsuffering;* 13 *Forbearing one*
> *another, and forgiving one another, if any man have*
> *a quarrel against any: even as Christ forgave you, so*
> *also do ye.* 14 *And above all these things put on charity,*
> *which is the bond of perfectness.* 15 *And let the peace of*
> *God rule in your hearts, to the which also ye are called*
> *in one body; and be ye thankful.*

See?! The Lord wants us His children to PUT OFF the things that cause us to act in murderous ways. Verses 8-9 require you to put OFF some things. Before you put on new clothes, you have to put off the old ones first. Then from verse 10 onwards we hear the things that we must put ON, with verse 14 capping it all . . . 'And above all these things *put on* charity, which is the bond of perfectness.' You see, you cannot kill someone you love. You cannot steal from the one you love. You do the best to the ones you love. Put on charity brother. Put on charity sister. After that, you act in love, filled with love, the Agape way.

So many people want new things. But I have also seen so many people who want BOTH the old and the new. So what would they rather do? They prefer to PUT ON the new clothes on top of the old ones. Now, you realise that is crazy. But crazy as it sounds, many people attempt to do this when it comes to spiritual things. They disregard the advice of **Col. 3** above, namely, PUT OFF first, then PUT ON. They would rather put on the new on top of the old. Imagine a person dressed like that. But I know that even when it comes to dressing, some people do that in the physical. I am not talking about dressing up with layers of clothing to deal with the elements of weather, as in when it is cold. I mean like putting on new underwear on top of old underwear, a new pair of trousers on top of an old one, or a completely new suit (jacket, tie, and all), on top of an old one! Now I am sure you agree: that is bizarre! Think of other examples. In my vernacular, they call it '*kuvirikidza*' or '*ukwelekanisa*'. What do you call it in your vernacular language?[16] Say it. You will understand it better that way.

What I know is that for people who do that, when the going gets tough, when things get hot one way or the other, if you have to take off something, guess what you will take off—the new ones of-course! Guess what you remain with. Yeah, you got it—the old clothes! The old garments. Your old self. You remain in the Church, but you have gone to your old self. Even you get confused by your own actions and behaviours. What you say is not what you wanted or meant to say. You do something and you wonder why on earth you did it. You don't know what came on you. You even think it's out of character! Well, check yourself. You did not put off first, the day you took on the new garment (salvation). Now is the time for redress. Put off first. Then put on Christ.
This right here is the serious problem affecting Christians today. I am sure by now you know what the Bible says in **II Cor. 5:17**:

> 17 *Therefore if any man be in Christ, he is a new creature: old things are passed away; behold, all things are become new.*

---

16 Let me repeat what I said earlier: I have come to realise that if things are said in one's native language, they tend to be grasped or understood better and quicker. So even in my preaching or sermons, if I go to countries whose first language or mother tongue is not English, I like to throw in a word or two in the native language. Often, I do that in the UK too. The response is always tremendous. So, if your first language is not English, please do interpret some of these words in your own mother tongue. My prayer is that one day this book shall be translated into many languages other than English, to benefit Christians all over the world.

The order remains the same. OLD things must pass away. Old clothes must go. Old habits must be put away. Thereafter, ALL things must become new. Put off the OLD, put on the NEW! Do exactly that, and see the new person you will be. Be filled with the Lord. Full of Christ. Ah! Church will be church! Our communities will be safer. Our countries will be full of tranquillity, when God's children are full of Christ, instead of the murderous spirits of jealousy and hatred. What fills you, control you.

CHAPTER SIX

Love/Charity

Love is another subject that has largely been misunderstood, misused or abused. It is one of those powerful things that fill mankind—and in the process controls many things people say and do. Let us look at the definition of love.

What is Love?

Love cannot be defined in one word, one phrase or one sentence. That's how powerful it is. When you love someone, you associate your love with words or phrases such as 'affectionate', 'passionate', 'fancy' 'attracted to', 'devoted', 'fondness', 'care for', and even 'adore', and 'worship'. Whichever of these words apply in your love for others, or for God, the saying in this book holds true: whatever fills you controls you.

The Four Love Kings

Research by numerous scholars found out that the Greeks identified four kinds of love; or rather four different motives for love. I shall refer to them as 'kings'. Since this book is not about love per se, I am just going to give a brief mention of the four 'love kings' here, so that we can assess to what extent each controls us humans and every living creature. Here we go.

i). KING "**EROS**".

Eros is the Greek word for sexual or carnal love. This word was not actually used in the New Testament, it is only alluded to. It means physical passion; its gratification and fulfilment. It's part of nature. The origin of the word is the mythical Greek god 'Eros', the god of love. Inferred in many Old Testament scriptures, Eros is the only kind of love that God restricts to a one-man, one-woman relationship within the bounds of marriage (see **Gen. 4:1-2; 21:1-3; 29:20-21; 30:4-5; Songs of Solomon 1:13; 1 Cor. 7:25; and**

Eph. 5:31; Songs of Solomon 4:5-6; Songs of Solomon 7:7-9; Songs of Solomon 8:10;).

Everything 'erotic' stems from this kind of love. I mean, King Eros rules! He dominates the world. He runs the show. King Eros has prompted many people to write different books and magazines. He is found in films and on the internet. He is in every home and in every country. He is simply pleasure of the flesh. He is in almost everyone's mind, even if they may not talk about it. Almost all of God's creation participates in this kind of love, one way or another, and mainly for propagation or 'pleasure' purposes. Humans, animals, all kinds of creatures, birds, fish and even plants all engage in erotic love. Many human beings spend their life chasing after this kind of love. It is abused and misused a lot. King Eros is the sort of love many people celebrate on the so-called 'Valentine's Day', when they exchange candy, flowers and all sorts of other things.

Indeed, what fills you controls you. When people are filled with this love king, well, you know what happens. King Eros has many casualties of different kinds. When were you last full of this kind of love? Would you tell us? When you were full of King Eros, how did he control you? No-one stands a chance of resisting this love King when he arrives. He takes over. He dominates. He takes complete control of all your senses—including common sense! He is another leveller. He takes complete control of kings and queens, rich and poor, etc

etc—you name it—all are subject to King Eros in the same way. Need I say more?

ii). KING "**PHILEO**".

Phileo is Greek for friendship love, a part of human nature. It is the love of the affections. It is delighting to be in the presence of another, a warm feeling that comes and goes with intensity. The most noted Phileo relationship in the Bible is that between David and Jonathan (see **I Sam. 18 and 19**). God never commands Phileo since this type of love is based on the feelings. Good, but flawed. However, almost all of God's creation enjoys King Phileo. Human beings and all kinds of creatures have friendships of one form or another. Dogs and lizards have friends. Birds and fish have friends. The list is endless. Male and female, young and old, poor or rich, educated or uneducated, black, pink, yellow or white; classify it anyway you want; all have friends. King Phileo in the house. There are different levels and bonds of friendship love. Some friends come and go, others stay longer, yet others never really go away, even if there is geographical distance. No doubt, when you are full of King Phileo, he also takes over. Friends, friends, friends! How many do you have? How much do you love them? How far can you go in the name of friendship love, King Phileo? You know what I am talking about. Many people 'go out of their way' (like Jonathan and David), to stand for each other under the influence of King Phileo. Well, this book is not about love, so I shall stop here.

iii). KING "**STORGE.**"

This is the third Greek word used for love. It refers to family love, also a part of human nature. Human beings and all kinds of God's creation belong to some family. Male and female, young and old, they all engage with each other on the basis of family love. Everyone needs to belong to some sort of family, to offer and receive comfort, support, companionship, fellowship and 'Storge'; family love. King Storge binds families together. When they are full of King Storge, you cannot come in between brother and sister, or brother and brother. When Cain slew his brother Abel (**Gen. 4**), he had allowed King Storge to emigrate, and in his place came the terrible twins, Jealousy and Hatred. The same thing had happened when Esau wanted to slay Jacob his brother (**Gen. 27:41**), and also when Joseph's brothers turned against him (**Gen. 37**). When he was now in a position to revenge, Joseph himself, full of King Storge, demonstrated true brotherly love (**Gen. 43:30; 45:14**). You see, as a human being you are not allowed to be a vacuum. If you are not full of one thing, you will be full of something else. And whatever it is that you allow yourself to be full of, that will surely control you!

iv). KING "**AGAPE**": THE KING of KINGS

The Greeks went on to identify and distinguish another, richer and deeper kind of love. They called it 'Agape', and I call it King Agape; the King of Love Kings! The Greeks defined this as divine love. Not part of human nature. This is God's kind of love. Agape—the

King of Kings. True, unconditional, unselfish love; love without justification. Jesus Christ used this word to describe the love of God for humanity. The Word of God teaches that this love is also possible between people. It is this kind of love that we need to acquire at this threshing floor level. Agape love is God's kind of love. Agape love seeks the welfare and betterment of others regardless of how one feels about them. In other words, Agape love does not have the primary meaning of feelings or affection.

This kind of love is so critical that God made it into a law. As part of the 'ten commandments', God commanded the children of Israel to love Him with all their heart, soul, strength, mind, and to love their neighbour as themselves. A certain lawyer made reference to this in **Luke 10: 25-29**. We were created to love God as He loves us; unconditionally; and to love our neighbours (i.e. our family members, brethren in the Church, colleagues and acquaintances at every level of social life) in the same way; unconditionally.

In pretty much the same way, and in keeping with the unity of the triune God, Jesus Christ emphasised it to His disciples, clearly demarcating it as a commandment, a law:

> *'A new commandment I give unto you, That ye love one another; as I have loved you, that ye also love one another. 35 By this shall all men know that ye are my disciples, if ye have love one to another'* **(John 13:34-35).**

In **John 15:12**, Jesus underlined King Agape even further:

> *'This is my commandment that you love one another, as I have loved you.'*

A commandment is law. It is not debatable. It is your duty. Duty should have nothing to do with feelings. If love has to do with feelings, it fits into the other three forms mentioned earlier, not here. Agape love, the commanded love, is and should always be without reference to feelings. In other words, the law of love in the Kingdom of God requires that you love your brethren first, then learn to like them afterwards. That's Agape, the King of all Love Kings.

Agape love should be unconditional. The moment someone attaches conditions or reasons to their love, then it's not Agape love. Danger warning signs are in the words "because" "as long as", "if," and "when" etc. Wherever there is a reason, there is a condition. Conditions create expectations, which may or may not result in disappointment. Agape means love without conditions, without boundaries, without justification or reasons. Oh, don't we all need this kind of love?!

The best earthly example of demonstration of Agape love is Joseph. He completely disregarded what his brothers had done to him previously. His full story is covered in the Bible, from **Gen. 30** (among other stories) through to **Gen. 50**. When King Agape, the King of all love Kings, is fully in you, he will perfect all the other kinds of love. The father in the story of the prodigal son (**Luke 15: 11-32**) is another scriptural example of Agape love in action. As you know, the brother who stayed at home was full of something else! The point here is that the other Love Kings are perfected by and through the 'King of Kings', Agape Love. Of course, God

Himself is Agape. God is love. He does not love us any other way. While we were yet sinners, God allowed his only begotten son, Jesus Christ, to die for us (**Rom. 5:8**). He did not wait till you were 'good', righteous or 'perfect'. If you are full of King Agape, you will demonstrate all the other kinds of love in their perfect sense. Allow Agape love, the King of Love Kings, to reign! Let me explain this same point further.

Love Kings Perfected in Agape

As I have alluded to above, please note that Agape love transcends or perfects the other three types of love. Eros, Phileo, and Storge kinds of love will all find fulfilment and perfection in someone who has Agape love first. Without Agape love, anyone who loves according to the other three Love Kings will be engaging in flawed kind of love, and usually ends in disappointment, heartbreak, resentment and all the rest of it. With God's kind of love (Agape, the King of Kings), someone is able to love their family (King Storge) and friends (King Phileo) in a most perfected way, and when one marries, the sexual love (King Eros) is then perfected. The end result is more satisfying, more fulfilled love and human relationships, home and away. Agape is top. Agape is the king of all loves, the king of kings!

The Love Kings in the Story of the Prodigal Son (Luke 15: 11-32)

In the book of Luke, on the passage quoted above, Jesus Christ tells a story that most people know. Bible scholars call it the story of 'The prodigal son'. Emphasis is put on the son who asked his father for a portion of his inheritance, went away to a far country, 'blew' it all, ended up destitute, till he 'came back to his senses' and went back home to be received in a grand way by his ever-loving father. Through this story, Jesus Christ wanted His disciples to appreciate the depth, length, breadth and height of our Heavenly Father's love. His unconditional love. His true agape! I do not want to sound like I am preaching here, but my view is that while the story is about agape love, it is perhaps a misnomer to call it 'The Prodigal Son'. Because then the emphasis is on the son who went away; the younger son. Yet it's a story about two sons.

In my view they were both prodigal in a way. It should perhaps be referred to as the story of 'The Prodigal Sons'. The son who went away demonstrated 'prodigality' through the act of going away from his father. Children, you do that at your own peril. Do not be greedy. Do not be selfish. Do not seek an advance of your inheritance. Be patient. After all you lack nothing in your father's house! Let the inheritance come at the right time, with the right (father's) blessing. Initially this boy was filled with greed. So greed controlled him; he asked for his portion and he left. Then, later on, he was filled with remorse and regret—and that controlled him all the way back home—back to his father's arms and love. When he went back, he was on the threshing floor[17]! Ok, everyone has

---

17 For a detailed read on this subject, please refer to 'Threshing Floor D.I.Y Style: A New Approach For A New Generation; From Harvest to Seed'; Dr. W. Masocha; Trafford, August 2013.

preached about this boy—the younger son who went away. So I shall leave him alone for now.

Well, the elder son who stayed at home also demonstrated 'prodigality' through his attitude, especially when his brother returned home. Perhaps he was even happy to see him go in the first place! Perhaps his spirit was rejoicing every time he heard of the sad plight of his brother in a far country. Here he was, all alone in the father's house, enjoying the father's attention, love and care; receiving the best on a daily basis. He does not even have an idea how many animals were slaughtered for him to enjoy in the house at the dinner table every day. Oh, he just took all that for granted. It was all his to enjoy, till the brother returned and spoiled his lonesome luxuries, his peace and quiet. When is your brother not your brother? What happened to family (Storge) love? Unless unconditional (Agape) love is present in a person, they struggle to love the 'Storge' (family) way. The prodigal son who remained at home proved it. He was full of arrogance and pride, anger and disdain. That controlled him full time. The story does not tell us that he eventually repented of his attitude. If he did not, then he missed paradise, yet he is the one who was in the father's house. OH!

Many in the church display a similar attitude to the boy who stayed at home. When someone who had backslidden, or had left the church, suddenly comes back, they are not very pleased to see that person being loved back by their spiritual father or by the senior leadership of the Church, or even by some saints. They should be isolated, alienated. They should be treated as a traitor, an outcast. Those without Agape love, that's what they will be thinking. You see, when you do not have the Agape love first, it is easy for jealousy and resentment to step in, with disastrous consequences for family, friends and church. But in the story of 'The Prodigal Sons', Jesus illustrated the true, unconditional (Agape) love as demonstrated by the father. He unconditionally received the son who had gone away, and unconditionally continued to love the son who had stayed at home. He did not berate him for his attitude, neither did he berate the other one for going away and wasting his wealth in a far country. There was no mention of the bad sides of the two boys, nothing. Only love, pure love. Unconditional love. But the elder brother was keen to point out his younger brother's faults (v. 28-30). Is this typical of brothers and sisters in your church? He was full of jealousy. Now you know what led him to speak and behave the way he did—Ah—what fills you controls you.

Oh, how I pray that all of us who call ourselves God's children should ensure we have the DNA of our Heavenly father! Yes, DNA. Are you your father's child? Do you pass the blood test? Do you carry your father's DNA? Whose child are you? Hey! Is God your father for real? Or are you a child of the devil? Sounds harsh? Well, read about Jesus's confrontation with the Pharisees in **John 8:37-44**. Your language, character, attitude and behaviour are perfect indicators of your genealogy. True children of God will love their brothers and sisters unconditionally if they are full of Agape. It's the only way. Jesus Christ is the way—the embodiment and personification of the Father's love. He is the only way! The King of Kings; Agape is the only way. Let all of God's children be full of this kind of love as individuals, as families, as communities, as Church, as a people, and as nations. That way we all contribute to making our world a better, happier, world. Let the King of Love Kings fill you today. Be filled with the unconditional love, the Agape kind of love.

True Love in the 'Mouth family'

Let me give you another practical example which demonstrates application of the King of Love Kings. One day I was sitting in my living room. I was thinking a lot about how best to apply Agape love. Then the Lord told me to look no further than my own mouth for the perfect example. The Holy Spirit told me to consider the mouth as a family; 'The Mouth family'. Consider this family as a home, or a church. In this family there are a number of brothers, responsible mainly for cutting and chewing food. We call these brothers 'Teeth'. Two identical sisters are at the front of the house. We call them 'Lips'. They have a big sister inside the mouth. She is called sister 'Tongue'. The roof of the house in the mouth family is called 'upper palette' in Biology, while the floor is called 'lower palette'. 'Saliva' is the oil that keeps the mouth family lubricated, making sure there is smooth flow, harmony and peace in the house.

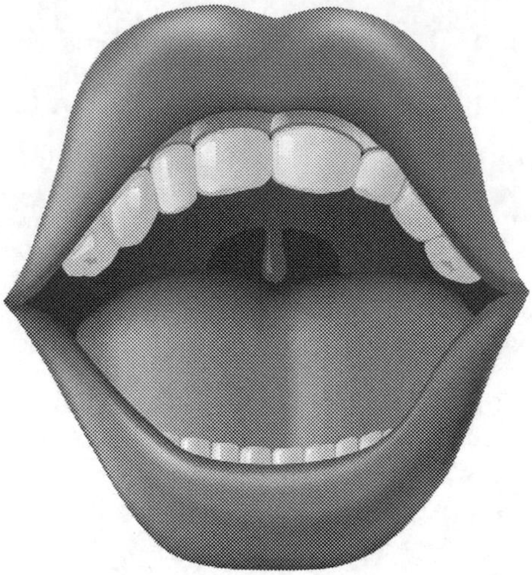

In a typical mouth family, occasionally one of the brothers, brother Teeth, collides with sister Tongue. Sometimes they collide with sister Lip. Usually when that happens, sister Tongue or sister Lip begins to bleed profusely. That's when you begin to see the Agape love in action. Everybody in the mouth family works hard to comfort the hurting one. Despite the obvious pain, there will be a lot of licking, cleaning and sympathy. All foreign objects are immediately dispatched away. Food will continue to be processed with tender, loving care. Despite the pain on the sister(s), inflicted by the brothers, the members of the mouth family continue to work together in true Agape (unconditional) love. No matter what has happened between them, they know that they will still need each other. They are quick to forgive each other. They are full of Agape love, and that love controls the way they relate one to another—even in the event of a disaster or major clash or disappointment in the family. It is true—what fills you controls you.

Let us continue to examine what happens in the 'Mouth Family'. Imagine you are having a meal, and it involves meat. As one will be taking meat, note that sometimes meat has a habit of depositing some of its smaller cousins in the space between the Teeth brothers. Watch the reaction of Sister Tongue. She will (without thinking or blinking) quickly run to the rescue of her brothers, and tries to behave like a toothpick! She works hard to remove the foreign objects. She does not have the spirit of revenge against brother Teeth. That's Agape in the mouth family! Pure, unconditional love. See what happens when members of your family, community, church or country are filled with the Agape kind of love?

The 'Love-O-Meter'

Please take your Bible and read **1st Corinthians 13!** Even if you know what it says—please read it again—read it now. You will be blessed. I call it **'The Love-o-Meter'**. Take your own readings at this great instrument of love. It measures how much and how well you love others. It also shows you which of the love kings dominates in your life. Check it out. Read verses 4-8 and see what score you get out of 16. How well do you do on God's Love-o-Meter? What readings do you get for yourself? You are Agaped if you get 16 out of 16, and nearly there if your reading is close to 16. No wonder this greatest chapter of love concludes at the 13th verse by saying:

> *'And now abideth faith, hope, charity (Agape kind of love), these three; but the greatest of these is charity.'*

Charity is the greatest. That's Agape love. Note that in this verse, if we look at it more deeply, we see that the three that remain or abide are representative of the trinity. Faith represents the Holy Spirit, Hope represents the Son, Jesus Christ, and Charity (Love) represents God the Father. It's an understatement when someone says 'God HAS love'. No. Not really. Not quite. I say, God IS LOVE! He is AGAPE! Agape is Love. Agape is King. Agape is the King of all Love Kings. Agape—the King of Kings. When He reigns, it rains! It rains until everyone is wet, until everyone is soaked in the latter rain of Agape love. Do you know the song that goes with these words. Well, go on—sing it then!

Love is a 'Doing Word'

When I was at junior school, I learnt a very important principle about love. I was taught that "Love is a verb", and that "A verb is a DOING word"! We should not just talk the language of love; children of God should learn to act, speak, think, and behave in love. Practical love. **Hebrews 10:24** requires that as children of God we should 'provoke' one another into only two things: love and good works. Whatever we say or do to others, as Christians, it should provoke the others only unto love and good works. When you are full of Agape love, your words, actions, behaviour, attitude etc should prompt others to doing good, and also to loving others as well. Agape Oh Yeah! Our Heavenly Father demonstrated his love for us. The most quoted verse in the Bible, **John 3:16,** sums it up:

> *"For God so loved the world, that he gave his only begotten Son, that whosoever believeth in him should not perish, but have everlasting life."*

Yeah, Agape love is the God-kind of love. It is for all 'whosoevers' out there. It is not selective. It is not judgmental. It has no strings attached. It makes no reference to race, colour, tribe or any other form of classification. It is completely without prejudice. God wants His children to show this kind of love one to another. Let God's children spread this kind of love. Agape. It is contagious. The King of Love.

Our Lord Jesus Christ, Himself the King of Kings and Lord of Lords, demonstrated this kind of love to us all, by agreeing to be the sacrificial lamb that paid all our debts and redeemed all of mankind. Oh, what manner of LOVE. For God so loved the world!

Our God reigns! True love reigns! Agape reigns! The King of all Love Kings, He reigns!! Let it rain! True Agape love is contagious. Let us be full of this kind of love. When the children of God are all full of the Agape kind of love, the King of Love Kings, they shall be in a position to spread it all over the world. Let God's children start an epidemic! Oh, come sing with me: '*Open the floodgates of Heaven. Let it rain . . . Let it rain . . .* !

CHAPTER SEVEN

Evil spirit(s); or Holy Spirit

The world we live in is divided into two kingdoms: the kingdom of God on the one hand, and the kingdom of the devil on the other. There are no in-betweens. As a human being, you are either controlled by the devil and his agents, or you are controlled by God and his angels. The two kingdoms are spirit-led. The spirit (or spirits) that control people from the devil are called evil spirits, whereas the Kingdom of God is controlled through the Holy Spirit. They are both spirit, the difference is that one is evil, the other is holy. Now, every individual is free to make a choice which of these spiritual realms should control their space. All living creatures can either be filled with the Holy Spirit or be filled with an evil spirit. Let us look at what happens when people and creatures are filled with evil spirits first.

Full of Evil spirits

For those who read the Bible, you may be aware of many examples where evil spirits manifested. Since the Bible is awash with such examples, I am just going to mention a few, just to drive the point home.

The Maniac: The story of Legion: The wisdom of the swine: Mark 5:1-20

Here is the well-known story of a man—a human being—who was possessed with (i.e. full of) evil spirits. The man was on self-destruction course. The evil spirits filled him, and were busy causing the man to inflict horrendous damage upon himself. Indeed it is true, what fills you controls you. This story is actually a demonstration of the respective powers of the two kingdoms; namely, the kingdom of the devil and the kingdom of God. The man was filled with evil spirits, lots of them—in-fact they were two thousand in number! (**Mark 5:13**). Then Jesus Christ—filled with the Holy Spirit—approached him. Note that it is not the man who was speaking to Jesus Christ. One of the evil spirits became the 'spokesman', answering on behalf of the other evil spirits resident in one man. The evil spirit confirmed that they were many, actually a 'legion' of them. Wow! It's amazing how many evil spirits a human being can accommodate! Seriously. One man had TWO THOUSAND evil spirits or demons in him!

The Bible says we wrestle not against flesh and blood, but against spiritual wickedness in high places (**Ephes. 6:12**). A very short spiritual contest ensued. Jesus filled with the Holy Spirit, face to face with a man filled with evil spirits. I am not going to repeat the story here. What followed the contest is that the evil spirits asked for permission to enter the flock of swine that was grazing nearby. You see, evil spirits cannot survive without a body. Note also that Jesus never killed or destroyed any demons or evil spirits, He just cast them out. That means by nature, evil spirits move from one living creature (human being or not) to another. Oh, please do be careful. Watch that evil spirits that are cast from one person do not end up lodging in you!

Anyway, so the evil spirits were granted their wish to enter the swine. Watch again the drama that followed. True to the principle of this book (what fills you controls you), as soon as the swine were filled with these evil spirits, they began to behave funny. They knew they can't swim, but all of a sudden they all rushed into the sea—and of course they all drowned! What a loss to the chap who owned them! I wonder what his reaction was when he was told what happened to his flock of swine! The whole flock perished just like that, because they were filled with evil spirits. I would dare say even further: credit to the swine. One pig could not contain one evil spirit, so decided that it was better to drown than to have an evil spirit and then pass it on to their young ones. All the pigs made this decision, the whole two thousand of them![18] Yet one man contained the whole lot!

18 Those who don't eat pork products cite this story as one reason why they don't eat pig meat. They say it was made dirty by evil spirits. I have some questions for people who think like that: First of all, what happened to the evil spirits after the swine died? Obviously they did not stay in the dead bodies of swine. Perhaps they went into the fish and other creatures of the sea! Secondly, the pigs affected were two thousand, based in Israel, near Galilee. Clearly the evil spirits did not enter the pigs in other parts of Israel and the middle east, England, Scotland, USA, Africa and other parts of the world. So why not enjoy their meat? Food for thought!

Ah! *Maiwee*! What does that say of us mortals? You see, animal or mankind, the saying is true: what fills you controls you.

Saul, filled with an evil spirit (see 1st Sam. 19:9)

If you are not full of the Holy Spirit, you will be filled with an evil spirit. You see, a human being is not supposed to exist as a spiritual vacuum. In this rather sad story, king Saul would make efforts to kill young David whenever the evil spirit was upon him. He would clutch a javelin, and throw it at him: attempted murder! Not surprising, eh, given that he was full of an evil spirit. Spirits are no respectors of persons. A king can be full of the Holy Spirit, and can also be full of evil spirits. Be careful of your environment. It dictates what spirit fills you. Well, now you know what happens when you are full.

Other people filled with evil spirits.

Over the years, I have had the privilege of serving God's people in many parts of the world, especially in Africa, UK, USA and Canada. I have witnessed countless incidences of the contest between evil spirits and the Holy Spirit. I have witnessed many people behaving in all sorts of weird ways under the control and influence of the evil forces of darkness. It was always such a joy and relief to see the same people back in their normal senses after the evil spirits had left them. They call it Deliverance. I am sure you know what I am talking about. I don't know about you, but I would not want ever to be filled with anything other than the Spirit of God, the Holy Spirit. Having read this book this far, I think you now know why.

Full of the Holy Spirit/Ghost

Obviously the Bible has countless examples of what happens when people are full of the Holy Spirit. Earlier on in the book, we looked briefly at **Ephesians 5:18** which says:

> *18. And be not drunk with wine, wherein is excess; but be filled with the Spirit;*

This scripture discourages being filled with wine (beer/alcohol/liquor), and encourages being filled with the Holy Spirit. I am sure you now know why. The Bible says in **Joel 2:28-30**:

> [28] *And it shall come to pass afterward, that I will pour out my spirit upon all flesh; and your sons and your daughters shall prophesy, your old men shall dream dreams, your young men shall see visions:*[29] *And also upon the servants and upon the handmaids in those days will I pour out my spirit.*[30] *And I will shew wonders in the heavens and in the earth, blood, and fire, and pillars of smoke.*

See what God promised His children? God wants all age groups and all flesh to be filled with His Spirit, for the world to see much demonstration of Divine power. Oh, Lord, do pour out your Holy Spirit upon me! Fill me now, in the mighty name of Jesus Christ!

See what God said to Moses about Bezaleel, of the tribe of Judah (**Exodus 31:1-5**):

> [1] *And the LORD spake unto Moses, saying,*[2] *See, I have called by name Bezaleel the son of Uri, the son of Hur,*

> *of the tribe of Judah:[3] And I have filled him with the spirit of God, in wisdom, and in understanding, and in knowledge, and in all manner of workmanship,[4] To devise cunning works, to work in gold, and in silver, and in brass,[5] And in cutting of stones, to set them, and in carving of timber, to work in all manner of workmanship.*

You need to be full of the Holy Spirit even to be a successful craftsman and businessman.

Again, we have many examples of people who did marvellous things under the control of the Holy Spirit. Consider the following few:

- **Luke 1:41:** *And it came to pass, that, when Elisabeth heard the salutation of Mary, the babe leaped in her womb; and Elisabeth was filled with the Holy Ghost:*

  What happened next? She was immediately transformed from an ordinary housewife into a prophetess! Holy Ghost power!

- **Luke 1:67:** *And his father Zacharias was filled with the Holy Ghost, and prophesied, saying,*

  Same thing happened to Zecharias, a priest who probably had never prophesied before! Filled with the Holy Ghost, the old man suddenly became a prophet! Wow! I sit.

- **Acts 1:8** says: *But ye shall receive power, after that the Holy Ghost is come upon you: and ye shall be witnesses unto me both in Jerusalem, and in all Judaea, and in Samaria, and unto the uttermost part of the earth.*

This is God's promise to the believers. When you are full of the power of the Holy Ghost, you become effective, local, regional and international soul-winners! When you are full of the Holy Ghost, you fulfil the Great Commission. Plundering hell, to populate Heaven!

- **Acts 2:4 says:** *And they were all filled with the Holy Ghost, and began to speak with other tongues, as the Spirit gave them utterance.*

See? When you are filled with the Holy Spirit, then you can speak in tongues. Do you speak in tongues? Are they real?

- **Acts 4: 8:** *Then Peter, filled with the Holy Ghost, said unto them, Ye rulers of the people, and elders of Israel,*

Also consider:

- **Acts 4:31:** *And when they had prayed, the place was shaken where they were assembled together; and they were all filled with the Holy Ghost, and they spake the word of God with boldness.*

Only the Holy Ghost gives you boldness to preach the gospel of the good news, the gospel of Christ, the gospel of the Kingdom of God.

- **Acts 7: 55-56:** 55 *But he, being full of the Holy Ghost, looked up stedfastly into heaven, and saw the glory of God, and Jesus standing on the right hand of God,* 56 *And said, Behold, I see the heavens opened, and the Son of man standing on the right hand of God.*

They stoned Stephen, but he remained full of the Holy Ghost to the bitter end. See the reward he got. He was the first and only human being to see the position of Jesus Christ in heaven. It gets better. The Bible tells us that Jesus Christ, when He ascended into heaven, He sat at the right hand of God the father (**Mark 16:19**). But in this instance, Stephen saw Jesus Christ standing on the right hand of God. This suggests to me that for what Stephen did, Jesus Christ (and probably God the father) gave him (Stephen) a standing ovation. My, oh my! Getting a standing ovation from the Divinity! Awesome!

- **Acts 10:38:** *How God anointed Jesus of Nazareth with the Holy Ghost and with power: who went about doing good, and healing all that were oppressed of the devil; for God was with him.*

  You see, Jesus Christ did the miracles etc, not just because He was the son of God, but because He was the son of Man full of the Holy Spirit. Do you get it?

- **Acts 13:9:** *Then Saul, (who also is called Paul,) filled with the Holy Ghost, set his eyes on him,*

  You don't want to know what Paul did to the Jewish sorcerer, Elymas, aka Bar-Jesus, do you? Well, you can only do what Paul did if you are full of the Holy Spirit. Then you are able to discern the evil spirits and deal with them appropriately. Don't do God's work without the Holy Spirit! *Unokuvara*!

Well, the Bible is awash with examples. I shall stop here, as far as examples are concerned.

God wants all of His children to be controlled only by the Holy Spirit. No surprise there! There is a story in **Ezek. 47:1-7** which demonstrates various stages of the infilling of the Holy Spirit. Please read the scriptures so you understand better what I am saying here. Now, let me give you an illustration, based on based on the same passage of scripture.

First of all, take a (say, between three to five litre) glass jar/jug/mug of water. Nicely put stones of various sizes in it, till it is full. Next, pour water into the jar, till it overflows. Can you tell how much water will be in the jar? Next step. Pour out the water into a smaller glass container (say a one litre bottle or a water glass). You will probably find that the water from the big jug with stones in it does not even fill up the water glass. That is evidence of how little water there was in the bigger jug, yet it looked full—in-fact it was overflowing! Now, go back to the bigger jug/mug. Remove all the stones. Take the smaller water glass and pour its water back into the bigger jar. What will you find? It barely covers a third of the jug! Ok, go on. Fill the jar with water. Now it is really full of water. When it had the stones, and you poured water to its brim, it appeared full, yet it was not!

The point is: when you allow impurities and other undesirable implements inside of you, you cannot be really full of the Holy Spirit. Real infilling is only possible when there are no stones. May God help us all to remove the impediments (stones) of sin in our lives and allow the Holy Spirit to properly infill us. When we are full of the Spirit of God, we do exploits for the Kingdom of God. Ask God to fill you. Be filled today—be filled with the Holy Ghost!

CHAPTER EIGHT

Conclusion

There are so many things that control the character and behaviour of man. I have come to the conclusion that no-one ever just does things without a controlling force behind. Nothing just happens. There is a force behind everything done or said by man under the sun. That includes creatures too.

Without filling the bread mixture with yeast, the flour will not rise in the oven, giving an undesired outcome of the baking process. Farmers fill up a cultivated piece of land with manure and fertilisers, and that chemical stuff suddenly controls the germinated plant, and it starts to flourish. If you fill a balloon with helium gas it suddenly runs away from your hands and zooms up in the air. On the other hand, if a human being fills themselves up with a helium gas called anger, before you know it there will be destruction all over the place. Farmers also use pesticides to deal with the insects and other things that damage their crop. What do they do? They simply fill up the local environment with a spray of the chemical, and within a short while all the pests within breathing distance of the spray begin to fill up with the stuff, and it controls them all the way to a sudden death. I could go on and on.

In this book I highlight what happens when we mortals allow ourselves to be filled by certain elements, which end up controlling (affecting) the way we speak, the way act, and the way we behave. I mean, these things have no respect for class, authority, position, title or whatever. They tend to control mankind in pretty much the same way. I call them 'levellers'. They bring anyone who is filled by them to the same level in terms of language, action and behaviour. I know there are a lot more 'substances' and things that fill and control mankind. I just picked a few in this book to highlight the whole point of the book: what fills you, controls you.

With various practical examples, I looked at the following:

- Pregnancy
- Alcohol and Drugs
- Bitterness and Anger
- Jealousy and Hatred
- Love/Charity
- Evil spirit(s)
- The Holy Spirit/Ghost

Well, you can see this is a small list of things that control anybody, as long as they allow them to infill them. These and other things, as I said earlier, are what I call ***levellers***. They take charge of whosoever! They do not care whether someone is rich or poor, educated or uneducated, king/prince(ss) or pauper, male or female, young or old, 'black or white', or whatever classification you may make. They have no respect for such human forms of classification. Once you allow these things to take up space inside of you, they immediately take over. They are in charge. They take control of the way you think, the way you speak, the way you act, and the way you behave. Whatever fills you controls you. True saying, that! Look at the above list again. Consider them one by one.

Well, you tell me then . . . . ;

WHAT ARE YOU FULL OF?